Education By Degrees

Masonic Notes

Raymond Apple

authorHOUSE®

AuthorHouse™ UK Ltd.
500 Avebury Boulevard
Central Milton Keynes, MK9 2BE
www.authorhouse.co.uk
Phone: 08001974150
Standard non-fiction disclaimer:
This book is a work of non-fiction. Unless otherwise noted, the author
and the publisher make no explicit guarantees as to the accuracy of
the information contained in this book and in some cases, names
of people and places have been altered to protect their privacy.

First published by AuthorHouse 9/13/2012

ISBN: 978-1-4772-2334-5 (sc)
ISBN: 978-1-4772-2335-2 (e)

Table of Contents

FOREWORD

This is not my first Masonic book. A much larger work of mine, "Freemasonry: Studies, Speeches, Sensibilities", was published in 2010 in print and electronic versions by the Museum of Freemasonry in Sydney. A follow-up collection of essays seemed almost inevitable once I took my own advice to engage in daily advancement in Masonic knowledge. I find the history and meaning of Freemasonry an inexhaustible fountain of fascination, and I hope my readers will discover something new about themselves as Masons as they move from one page to the next. I am still far from certain that I have the *answers* to all my Masonic questions, but I am beginning to understand the *questions*. Most of the contents of this book, though they represent one man's take on a difficult series of subjects, are written from a factual and objective point of view, though almost every chapter has a personal and possibly idiosyncratic tinge. As with all my Masonic researches and writings I warmly thank my friend Right Worshipful Brother Joe Haffner for encouraging me and pointing me in the right direction. I am also most grateful to the generous sponsors who have made this publication possible, though neither they nor any Lodge or Grand Lodge bear responsibility for my views and opinions.

RAYMOND APPLE

Jerusalem, 2012

THE MAJOR SPONSOR OF THIS BOOK IS LODGE
MARK OWEN NO. 828 OF SYDNEY, AUSTRALIA

THE AUTHOR

Raymond Apple is a rabbi who was a leading figure in Australian public life for many years. His 45-year Masonic career has covered Britain, Australia and Israel. He is Past Deputy Grand Master of the United Grand Lodge of New South Wales and the Australian Capital Territory.

1. A HOUSE NOT BUILT WITH HANDS

I have known Masons who walked through the streets muttering the craft ritual to themselves. Not necessarily because they were rehearsing a Masonic charge, but because they found the traditional wording so poetic and inspiring. Characteristically, the wording is about mortality and morality, buildings and builders, ethics and attitudes.

One of the finest Masonic phrases is the reference to "a house not made with hands". Probably deriving from the beginning of Isaiah Chapter 66 in the Hebrew Scriptures, it appears a number of times in the New Testament, notably Acts 7:48, Hebrews 9:11 and II Corinthians 5:1. It parallels the earthly temple "made with hands" – one of the greatest products of the ancient building trade – with a spiritual temple "eternal in the heavens". The contrast is important in the controversies of the first century BCE and first century CE concerning the role and status of the earthly temple. Stephen, later to be stoned to death as the first Christian martyr, argued with his contemporaries that "the Most High does not dwell in houses made with hands; as the prophet (Isaiah 66:1-2) says, 'Heaven is My throne and earth my footstool; what house shall you build for Me? says the Lord; what is the place of My rest? Did not My hand make all these things?'" (Acts 7:48-50).

The founders of Masonic ritual named their meeting places "temples", but they taught that the wider task of the Mason was to make the whole creation a temple to God. The Jewish philosopher Philo of Alexandria wrote (*Special Laws* 1:66-67), "In the highest and truest sense the holy temple of God is the whole universe".

A quite different approach was taken by some who thought of heaven as a temple that awaited us upon death, implying that this life was not nearly as desirable as that of the hereafter. Isaac Watts' famous Hymn 110 declares,

"There is a house not made with hands,
Eternal and on high;
And here my spirit waiting stands
Till God shall bid it fly.
Shortly this prison of my clay
Must be dissolved and fall;
Then, O my soul! with joy obey
Thy heav'nly Father's call."

Freemasonry is not a theology or religious denomination, and it expresses no view about whether death is better than life. It notes that Ecclesiastes, which provides (Chapter 12) some of the wording for the third degree ritual, asserts that the day of death is better than the day of birth (Chapter 7), but it leaves it to a Mason's own religious tenets to decide whether Watts, and Ecclesiastes, ought to be endorsed.

In the meantime no-one can argue with the Masonic proposition that the ethics and attitudes learnt in the Lodge room ought to accompany a Mason along every path in life and help to construct a quality society: another way of saying that with the aid of the principles of the Craft the whole world can become a temple that is made not by builders' hands but by the invisible virtues of love, respect, compassion and concern.

A technical note: BCE = Before the Common (or Christian) Era, CE = Common Era

2. BRINGERS OF LIGHT

Light is a major Masonic symbol. Entering upon his Masonic career at a dramatic moment of awareness, a new Brother is asked what he most desires, and he spontaneously answers "Light". His introduction to the craft teaches him the profoundest lesson that Freemasonry has to teach, that life can be a vale of darkness and gloom unless a person can find a way through. Amidst what sounds like a clap of thunder, he hears the Biblical words (Gen. 1:2-4), "And God said, 'Let there be light'… and there was light". Something suddenly tells him that every great truth comes like a flash of light. No wonder Cecil Rhodes, on his death bed, called out, echoing Goethe, "Licht, mehr Licht! (Light, more light!)"

In the days of Operative Masonry, work was more or less restricted to the daylight hours when the sun was shining, though at night people probably had some form of torch or lamp because otherwise no-one could see where they were going. They emulated the Israelites in the wilderness, led by "a pillar of cloud by day to show them the way, and a pillar of fire by night" (Exodus 13:21-22, Nehemiah 9:12).

Speculative Freemasonry allegorised the pillars of light. It spoke of "emblematical lights" and borrowed a phrase from Milton ("Paradise Lost", 1:59), who wrote about "darkness visible" which revealed only "sights of woe".

It could suggest our uncertainty about what lies after our earthly life – or it could be taken as a reference to life on earth itself, where so much remains beyond our mind's reach. The ritual refers to "that mysterious veil which the eye of human reason cannot penetrate... unless assisted by THAT LIGHT which is from above".

The Masonic concept of light from above was once described in the ritual in Christian terms as Father, Son and Holy Ghost, though this was later recast in more generalised language. Or possibly some Enlightenment-era Freemasons were not conventionally religious, and thought "from above" was a hint of high-minded human reason.

Every flash of light needs a source. Matthew Arnold said that the Israelites were bringers of light - the prophet Isaiah called them "a light unto the nations" (Isaiah 49:6) – whilst the Philistines brought darkness. This is why anticulturalism is called Philistine.

In their own way Freemasons are and see themselves as bringers of light.

Lodge rooms always made a point of being well lit – originally with three large candles which ensured that the brethren would see the ritual properly, but were subsequently accorded a symbolic significance.

As symbols, there emerged two sets of lights, three

"great" lights (the Volume of the Sacred Law, the square and the compasses) and three "lesser" lights (the sun, the moon and the Worshipful Master).

The sun and moon gave physical light and ensured that no-one would grope and stumble; the WM personified order and stability. The VSL, square and compasses were "great lights" because they suggested how to choose the right path in life.

Freemasonry dreamed of reaching Utopia. In European Freemasonry the craft used the term "bringing of light" to denote the spread of Masonic tradition. In recent years, when the Hungarian Grand Lodge was re-established, it was said that "the light was brought from Germany and Austria". But in a broader sense the craft saw itself as a bringer of light even to the so-called "profane" outsider.

3. CHINA AND THE MASONIC ARCHIVES

I have no idea whether China has any Masonic lodges, but when I visited Beijing and saw ancient stone pillars bearing historical records I recalled the passage in the ritual which claims that our ancestors placed their records on (or in) columns to keep them safe.

The Bible is the source of this idea. Moses was told (Deuteronomy 27:2), "When you cross the Jordan to the land which the Lord your God gives you, you shall set up great stones and cover them with plaster, and you shall write upon them all the words of this law". Joshua 8:32 reports the implementation of this command: "And he wrote there upon the stones a copy of the law of Moses". Many ancient cultures had a similar idea. The Code of Hammurabi was inscribed on hard stone to give it durability. In the Louvre in Paris one can still see the result, which long outlived Hammurabi himself.

The purpose of stone archives was not only to ensure

their survival but to make them available to the people. Not everybody could read and write, but those who were literate could never argue ignorance of the law. The Bible made this clear when it said, "Moses commanded us a law, an inheritance of the congregation of Jacob" (Deut. 33:4).

As often happened, Freemasonry embellished the notion with a story. It averred that the children of Lemech (see chapter 23 of this book) feared that the world would be engulfed by destruction by fire or flood, and whatever branches of knowledge early man developed (as inferred from the early chapters of Genesis) would be lost. They "took counsel together" and inscribed all the principles of the sciences of the time upon pillars, one made of material that would survive burning, and one that would survive water.

In this way human knowledge was transmitted inviolate from generation to generation and Freemasonry gained one of its great symbols – the pillars which feature so prominently in Masonic architecture and Lodge room design.

King Solomon's Temple had, according to the Bible, a pillar on each side of the entrance, one named Boaz and one Yachin (I Kings 7:21-22; II Chronicles 3:17, Jeremiah 52:20-22). Masonic ritual thought these names were in honour of two Biblical personages, Boaz, who was King David's ancestor, and Yachin, a Temple priest. In spite of Masonic claims to the contrary, this Yachin was of obscure rank and hardly worthy of commemoration. The truth is that the two pillars gained their names not because of any historical figures but because of their symbolism. "Boaz" is really "*b'oz*" – "in strength"; *Yachin* is "He will establish".

As the synagogue emulates the Temple in many

ways, the two pillars are frequently found as decorative features of the Ark (the repository of the scriptural scrolls) and its curtains. The Ark curtains probably derive from the screen that separated the *sanctum sanctorum* from the congregation.

If we understand the two pillars as inspired by the Moses story of pillars containing the Divine law, Boaz enshrines the message that real strength comes from God-given morality ("The Lord will give strength to His people" – Psalm 29:11) and Yachin that stability comes from firm principle. A Temple perpetuating God's teaching will stand; a nation founded on God's law will have true power. That is why an 18th century Masonic document speaks of "two essential and fundamental Pillars of all good Fellowship – TACITURNITY and CONCORD".

A technical note: Yachin is not pronounced Jarkin. Hebrew has no "J"; the "ch" is as in "loch".

4. TRUE BLUE MASONRY

Why is Freemasonry sometimes called "The Blue Lodge"? It can't simply be because in London the early lodges met at inns with "Blue" in their names, e.g. "The Blue Boar" and "The Blue Star". The choice of such hostelries for Masonic gatherings is only a coincidence, but it begs the question. Why should an innkeeper call his premises "blue" unless there was already a significance in the colour?

Blue is an important feature in Strine (the Australian lingo). A mistake is *a blue*. If you have a row with someone, that's *a blue* too. You carry your *bluey* on your back. Lest you think that blue doesn't figure outside Australia, consider that in many countries to waste your money is *to blue it* (or blow it – though whether blueing came before blowing, or vice-versa, I don't know). A Tory is *a blue*: so is a policeman. Surprises come *out of the blue*. When you depart you sail off *into the blue*. Dark blue is Oxford: light blue is Cambridge. If you represent one of these ancient universities in sport and wear the university colour, you are an Oxford or

Cambridge blue. Brides are told, for no logical reason, to wear "something borrowed, *something blue*".

The use of colours to convey a message applies very widely. A novice is green, a Communist is a red, a coward is yellow. You can be green with envy and white with rage. But blue seems to be the king of colours. The Egyptians saw it as a sacred colour. The Babylonians gave their idols blue garments. The Druids said blue symbolised truth

A Masonic scholar, Fred Crowe, argued a century ago that Freemasonry adopted the blue of the Order of the Garter. His view is debatable, even though the craft claimed to be older and better than the Order of the Garter – but did the Order of the Garter itself give blue a cachet because of a lady's blue garter? There may be something in the thought that in the early 18th century blue was associated with the royal Stuarts. On the other hand, the Operative Masons of the Middle Ages probably had *white* aprons!

Blue has a universal symbolism in the cultures of the world. Not just because of pubs or garters, but because of the sea and sky. We don't need to be too pedantic about how to judge what colour the sea is, or the sky, but as ordinary laymen see it, the sky is blue and stands for constancy and optimism. Blue skies do more for human beings than grey ones. The sea also looks blue and stands for cleanliness and calm.

The rabbinic sages of Judaism went a stage further and said, "The sea reminds us of the sky; the sky reminds us of God".

For Freemasonry, then, influenced so greatly by Biblical and rabbinic imagery, blue represents fundamental virtues and the belief in the Creator, whom Freemasonry calls the Great Architect and Grand Geometrician of the Universe.

As a result it symbolises quality – true-blue, blue-ribbon, blue-blood.

It was not Freemasonry that chose blue; it was blue that chose Freemasonry. No other colour would have been as effective or educative.

Oxford blue, Cambridge blue, blue garters, Blue Boar inns… all arose out of the same origins, though Masonic blue is closer to the Oxford than the Cambridge version.

Long before I knew that my father was a Freemason or imagined that I would be one myself and have blue in my Grand Lodge regalia, my mother used to say blue – especially navy - was a serviceable colour, not showing the dirt but warmer and friendlier than black. Others call it a royal colour. Indeed it is, and it brings a touch of majesty into the Masonic regalia which I wear and use with such pride.

5. THE MASTER'S HAT

There was a time when Speculative Freemasons took it for granted that proper dress in Lodge included a hat. The practice probably began because wearing your hat in the street was axiomatic. Hats were even worn indoors, even at mealtimes. The reason seems to have been climatic. The uncovered head felt very cold, especially when men's full-bottomed wigs went out of fashion. Small wigs tied at the nape of the neck provided some protection but not much. When even these went out of fashion – probably because the powder with which they were dusted became too expensive owing to the "powder tax" that helped to finance the Napoleonic wars - it became normal for men to wear their own hair without a wig. However, because the hair was cut short, a man would wear something like a night-cap in the house and a cocked hat in the street.

At Lodge meetings there was no central heating, and not everybody could sit near the fire, so it helped to wear a hat. It is possible that someone rationalised the head covering by recalling that the ancient Romans prayed and attended sacrifices with covered head, provided they were free men... and the essence of the craft was that Masons were "free", whatever the reason for the term. I have also heard it said that wearing a hat was a sort of tyling, a reminder that the Lodge room was "tyled" to symbolise the roof being covered to keep the secrets in and the cowans out.

In time, the wearing of a hat in Lodge was restricted to the Worshipful Master as a mark of his authority and status. Ordinary people doffed their hats as a sign of respect to a superior... and in Masonic terms, the WM *was* the superior.

In Jewish practice the wearing of head covering completed one's dress and was regarded as a mark of humility in the presence of God. The Temple priests wore head covering, but the ordinary person did not need to, except as a sign of personal piety. Rabbinic literature claims that when the Israelite slaves left Egypt they showed their independence by boldly going out with heads uncovered, but later it became etiquette to wear a hat; a person who did not conform to this rule was considered a boor and in some circles even a thief.

It seems too that in the first century CE, children covered their heads out of respect for their teachers and elders, and so schoolboys sat in class with their caps on.

Christians removed the hat during prayer, which probably hardened the Jewish usage of deliberately covering the head in worship, though some Jewish groups still prayed with uncovered head in the Middle Ages.

Probably the only Masonic trace of these variations on a

theme is that a Jewish candidate takes his craft obligations with covered head. It is also customary for a Jew taking an oath in court to cover his head, though probably more important than the hat is the use of a Hebrew Bible.

Where Occidental custom advised covering the head both outdoors and inside by reason of the cold weather, Oriental custom recommended head covering for the opposite reason, to be protected against the hot sun.

Customs change. These days you never see a member of the House of Commons wearing his top hat in Parliament, nor does a Mason have his head covered in Lodge unless he is an orthodox Jew. The Master does not wear his hat in Lodge. Indeed most Masters do not even possess a hat.

6. DANCING WITH A SHIBBOLETH

The key words in Masonic ritual include "Shibboleth". You would think that no-one would find it hard to pronounce, but in Biblical times there were people who could not say a "sh". What they did if they wanted someone to be quiet I have no idea. We today would be lost if we couldn't *shoosh* somebody.

It seems that there was a real problem if you were an ancient Ephraimite being pursued by a Gileadite.

According to the Book of Judges, "The Gileadites took the fords of the Jordan against the Ephraimites, and it happened that when any of the Ephraimite fugitives said, 'Let me cross', the Gileadites said to him, 'Are you an Ephraimite?' If he said 'No', they said to him, 'So say *Shibboleth*', but he said *Sibboleth* because he could not pronounce it correctly, they seized him and slew him" (Judges 12:5-6).

The ability to say a "sh" was a test to establish who a

person was. By extension a shibboleth has become a word, phrase or idea which identifies a group.

It is said, with what credibility I don't know, that people with a Lithuanian Jewish background still can't say a "sh". If they try to say "B'reshis" (Genesis) they can't do better than "braces". If they are Yiddish-speakers and want to say "shiess!" ("shoot!") they end up with "cease!"

There are other linguistic problems that a number of nations have. Some can't pronounce "l": others can't say "r". It makes it particularly hard for people who are trying to learn English.

Australians sometimes identify each other by means of the word Woolloomooloo. Think how hard that word would be if you came from a place where they couldn't pronounce the letter "l". New Zealanders are known (and sometimes mocked) for saying what sounds like "fersh and cherps" instead of "fish and chips". The Irish Catholic teaching nuns instructed their pupils to say "haitch" instead of "aitch".

The actual origin of "shibboleth" is a Hebrew word for an ear of corn or a spring of water. A graceful Israeli folk dance is "*Shibbolet Ba-Sadeh* – A shibboleth in the field".

But back to shibboleth in the sense of a trait that marks out a group. A respected rabbi told me that in his view, certain fundamentalist colleagues were making a shibboleth of small issues in religious doctrine.

In a less exalted realm, think of the television show "Keeping Up Appearances". Hyacinth Bucket has the shibboleth of insisting that the surname is pronounced "Bouquet" – and another shibboleth of constant social climbing and appearing to be upper-crust. I suppose that her husband Richard has his own shibboleth of letting his wife get away with it and believing that the way to maintain a marriage is two words – "Yes, dear!"

In Masonic teaching, shibboleth symbolises plenty. In broader human culture it gives people plenty of trouble.

7. FREEMASONS AND THE INNER TEMPLE

Playing "Monopoly" was part of my childhood. It introduced me to buying and selling, though I never developed any great skill at either. It also taught me the geography of London, and at that it succeeded so well that I had a constant sense of *déjà vu* when I eventually came to England and lived in London for fifteen years.

I had already been a law student in Melbourne and dreamt of becoming a barrister with a connection to the Inner or Middle Temple. I had no idea why there should be places in London with those names; it did not seem to have anything to do with the Temple in ancient Jerusalem. My confusion only increased when I became a Freemason and discovered that Masonic meeting places were also generally called temples.

The London part of the problem was solved when I found that London and Paris both had buildings that had belonged to the Templars and one of the London buildings became the headquarters of part of the legal profession.

The Templars were a military religious order, Knights of the Temple of Solomon, founded by the Crusaders early in the 12th century. Since their order began in Jerusalem, it did not surprise me to find a Templar cemetery in Emek Refa'im not far from my present Jerusalem home.

From a now deceased senior Freemason, the late Charles Aaron, I acquired a set of *Mackey's Encyclopedia*, which informed me (vol. 3, page 1207), that "after the Bible began to be published in cheap editions, and especially in illustrated form, a passion for the Book spread rapidly across England, and with it began a wide popular interest in Solomon's Temple; that interest was greatly heightened by the display at two different times of large-scale models of the Temple in London".

Freemasonry fostered an interest not only in the design and construction of the Jerusalem Temple but in King Solomon and his court, and urged members of the craft to take charge of their lives like a Solomonic project manager, and to become living temples of the virtues.

However, calling their meeting places temples tended to produce negative attitudes to Freemasons and their movement. Critics saw it as evidence that we were setting ourselves up as a rival religion and undermining the Christian denominations (some even said we were satanic!), so in some places there was a gradual abandonment of the name "temple" in favour of terms such as "Masonic Centre".

In 1987 when the Grand Master of the United Grand Lodge of New South Wales asked the Board of General

Purposes to undertake the major task of removing the word Temple from the Masonic landscape, my friend the late Sir Asher Joel was amongst senior members of the craft who profoundly disagreed with the decision, arguing in a letter addressed to the Grand Secretary that it constituted a "deviation from the established Customs and Ancient Landmarks of the Order".

I am not certain that I feel quite as strongly as this. I admit that our use of the word Temple could give a wrong impression, but it does not worry me to change the designation of our meeting places so long as the ethical teachings built around King Solomon's Temple are maintained and we continue to aspire to build the whole world into a temple of moral values and to dedicate our lives to Masonic virtues.

In that sense I have finally realised how to become a member of the Inner Temple without needing to be a practising lawyer.

8. AT VARIANCE

Everyone who joins the Masonic craft is adjured that if he is at variance with a Brother who is present in Lodge they should try to sort out their differences before the atmosphere of the Lodge room is affected. It is deemed better not to enter a meeting at all if a relationship problem would disturb the harmony of the Lodge.

I recall only one occasion when objections were raised to the admission and affiliation of a Brother with whom leading members of my Lodge were at variance.

The Brother concerned arrived at a meeting and would not accept that there were objections to his presence. As he knew me and did not think I was amongst those who were at variance with him, he insisted that I come out of the meeting and talk to him. When the message was conveyed to me, the Worshipful Master agreed to my attempting to mediate - but my efforts were not successful, and the Grand Secretary wrote to the Brother asking him not to pursue his application for affiliation.

The incident illustrates how precious the harmony of a Lodge is to its members, but it doesn't tell us enough about what is meant by being "at variance".

It is obvious that people constantly disagree on many matters. We do not necessarily think alike, believe the same things, hold the same religious, political or economic opinions, or share the same interests and commitments. Does this constitute being "at variance" within the terms of Masonic ethics? Even if there are Brethren with whom we have had a serious disagreement and falling-out, is this what is meant by being "at variance"?

Whatever the procedural regulations of a Lodge or Grand Lodge have to say on the matter, I think the best approach is suggested by a passage in the writings of the theologian/ethicist Abraham Joshua Heschel. In his essay, "No Religion is an Island", Heschel says, "Should we refuse to be on speaking terms with one another and hope for each other's failure? Or should we pray for each other's health in preserving one's respective legacy...?"

Being at variance need not be a major issue unless we "hope for each other's failure". The question is whether despite our differences we can sit together and wish each other good health and success in all we undertake.

Heschel was concerned for the relationship between religions. In Heschelian terms, no religion should pray for the other to come a cropper. Each should wish the other success in being itself and "preserving (its) respective legacy".

In Freemasonry the success of mature Masons is whether they can say to each other, "Brother, you are my Brother. We are neither copies nor clones of each other. Our views and values may not be identical. But I wish you well, and I am sure you reciprocate".

This does not rule out the human propensity to exacerbate the atmosphere within a group or society – including a Masons' Lodge - nor our capacity to contain it if we really want to. But it does suggest how a Masonic conscience should define the question, "Are we really at variance?"

9. WOMEN IN THE LODGE

Why is official Freemasonry a male preserve, a men's club? It is part of a pattern. Social mores – until recently - kept women out of public life. The men went out to work; the women were relegated to what used to be called "home duties". This only changed during wartime when most of the men were away and women took over many of their jobs; and when women gained more control over their sexuality.

There were always organisations through which women undertook good works – mothers' clubs, ladies' guilds, women's auxiliaries, Dorcas societies and others, but they lacked the status of men's clubs including Masonic lodges.

Strangely, men adopted what seemed like women's dress in certain areas of activity - not only Masonic aprons but professional robes and gowns for barristers, judges and clergy, though they still excluded the women themselves from these roles.

In operative Masonry there was a view that women lacked the strength and stamina for hard physical labour, which would have been especially hard for women during menstruation and pregnancy. Speculative Freemasonry ruled, "The persons admitted members of a Lodge must be good and true men... no bondmen, no women, etc." There may even have been a feeling that women were incapable of intellectual activity.

There are stories, how true we cannot be certain, of a woman (said to be a Miss St. Leger) gatecrashing a Lodge meeting (possibly in County Cork) and then being hurriedly initiated in order to keep the craft's secrets intact. This is said to be the reason why the first degree ritual came to contain a test which prevented the admission of "an imposter as to sex, our rules forbidding the introduction of females into our ceremonies".

Some groups of women found this offensive and invented women's and co-Masonry. Women's Orders tended to formulate a series of degrees and ceremonies reminiscent of Freemasonry, though they sometimes featured Biblical women rather than men. They were generally independent of any establishment Grand Lodge. In official Lodges the women were merely the tea ladies, though the men occasionally deigned to allow ladies' nights - social functions at which women were allowed to be present.

I confess that one of the few occasions when my brother Freemasons robustly attacked me was at a Masonic convention in North Queensland where I suggested that we develop unisex lodges. I was told very plainly that it would never work, not that anyone could find or quote a problem of principle against it but because the men felt their wives would be up in arms. What, I was asked, would happen to Masonic marriages if a Brother sat in lodge next to an attractive woman who happened to be someone else's wife?

In France in the 18th century there were aristocratic lodges for Masons' wives, daughters and sisters (Gilbert and Sullivan might have borrowed from this the phrase, "his sisters and his cousins and his aunts") but these Lodges of Adoption were not unisex in the sense I was thinking of and they disappeared from the scene of history until a revival in the 1930s and 40s.

I still think that joint lodges would be a good idea. Of course there would need to be considerable rethinking of our ritual and terminology. The opening up of the craft to female members would not necessarily appeal to the whole craft but would be a matter of local option, though because Freemasonry is a disciplined movement it would need the full approval and understanding of the relevant Grand Lodge.

10. WHAT'S TO EAT?

Operative masons were generally away from home for years on end, working on big building projects that required considerable skill and a large labour force. Near the work site was the lodge (for more details see chapter 22 – "Where You Lodge") which housed the team of workmen, and after dark when work had ceased for the day they talked together, ate together and probably sang ballads together. What they ate depended on who knew how to cook and what ingredients were available. Presumably the menu was rich in red meat and deficient in fruit and vegetables. They drank wine, mead or water. Apart from their diet, they would have led a relatively healthy life because of all the fresh air and exercise, but in those days life expectancy was unlikely to have been high, and some men never made it back home again.

Things became quite different with the advent of Speculative Freemasonry. Not only did the movement appeal to the better-fed upper classes and the educated sectors of society, rather than the rough-and-ready tradesmen who worked on building sites, but the meetings were often in public houses where the food was of better quality. We have considerable archival records of what these inns served and charged. Indeed, the minute books show that Lodges sometimes threatened to take their custom elsewhere where they would get a better deal.

Over the years the after-meeting supper – sometimes called a South because that part of the encampment was where the Operatives had their lodging house - became a regular feature of Lodge meetings. It is not so much that the Brethren needed a solid meal, though some came straight from work, but the convivial atmosphere created a sense of fellowship and made the meeting into a social occasion.

I have sat at countless Lodge suppers ranging from elegant catered dinners at the Cafe Royal in Piccadilly to slapdash servings of meat and potatoes that Brethren told me were only palatable because of the alcohol that came with them. There were temperance Lodges where alcohol was supposed to be banned, but sometimes a little ingenuity got around the ban and you could easily smell the result.

Personally I rarely eat at the festive board. I not only keep *kosher* but I don't eat meat, so unless the Lodge orders a *kosher* vegetarian meal for me I nibble on nuts, feed on fruit or simply excuse myself and go home. In any case I have my meal at a regular hour at home so when I arrive at Lodge I am not really hungry.

But I have my doubts as to whether the way we run the after-meeting eating experience does us any good. If it has no class or style, we would be better off limiting ourselves to a drink (including tea or coffee) and a piece of cake, possibly accompanied by nuts, crisps, olives, cut-up fruit and vegetables.

We already lose more than enough members who slip through the cracks because Lodge meetings are a bore to them, because there is no non-ritual program worth the name, no-one seems to keep in touch, it all looks like a geriatric club, and the membership fees are probably way too high. Why add sloppy catering and unattractive food to the reasons why people give up on Freemasonry? Why not make our Lodges more interesting, more affordable, more elegant - and more appetising?

11. MAKING THE TOAST

A dear friend whose husband served as a rabbi in various countries arrived in Newcastle, Australia, not knowing much English, and was invited to a civic event at which they wanted to honour her with giving a toast. She had no idea of the idiomatic connotation of the English word "toast", but she knew that toast was something you did with bread. So she carefully toasted countless slices of bread, wrapped them in a tea towel and brought them to the town hall at the appointed hour. Nobody laughed aloud, but she could see the grin on their faces and when her English improved she told and retold the story with great gusto.

Of course English is a funny language and words like "toast" are a source of puzzlement even to native English speakers. A toast with wine and no bread? Toast that needs a speaker and not a toaster? A crazy language.

"Roast" is an even more peculiar word. To toast someone is to honour them, often over-effusively; to roast them is to laugh at them and uncover their foibles, albeit in good humour and without any malice. It has nothing to do with meat, but we expect the victim to sit there like a lamb and sense that we have a beef about them. They can't be chicken and run away. A crazy language.

In Masonic social life, toasting is taken for granted. We toast the Grand Master, we toast the visitors, we toast whoever we can – is it because we welcome any excuse for a drink?

My dictionary tells me that to roast has an informal connotation of "to criticise severely", but since the subject of this article is toasting and not roasting we don't need to go into that. Toasting in the sense of paying a tribute may have a link with heat in that it shows a warm feeling. It has also been suggested that giving a toast may have begun as a mark of honour to a lady, and toasting her gave the wine an extra spice or flavour.

Roasting possibly began in an American context, and toasting in Britain. Personally I have no objection to either. I have been both *toasted* and *roasted*. If you will allow me to continue the rhyme, I hope I have never *boasted* too much.

I have to admit that at Masonic social gatherings the toasts are often hard to take, and the replies are even worse. Some people who give or respond to toasts are long-winded and don't know how to bring their words to a conclusion. Long-winded responses with the compulsory bad jokes are a trial. Telling a joke is an art, and very few people have mastered it. It is also a problem if the supposed joke turns out to be offensive and even racist.

I have some advice which I believe will help. Keep your toasts brief and your responses even briefer. Leave out the jokes. Stand up, speak up, shut up – the three ingredients of a good speech. I have an etymological dictionary that says, "Toast – see Torrid". Not a bad idea. Some toasts and responses are indeed torrid. Maybe you remember the saying, "Everyone thought he was a fool, and when he opened his mouth they all knew he was."

12. DUE EAST AND WEST

The first degree ritual makes the bold assertion that the orientation of the Lodge is due east and west. The Master of the Lodge is in the east: the Senior Warden is in the west. The emphasis on the east is said to have three reasons:

- the sun rises in the east and sets in the west;
- learning began in the east and spread to the west;
- the Israelite tabernacle in the wilderness of Sinai was due east and west.

What about the Jerusalem Temple? For theological reasons, its orientation was apparently westwards. Chapter 8, verse 16, of the Book of Ezekiel says: "At the door of the temple of the Lord, between the porch and the altar, were about twenty-five men with their backs toward the temple of the Lord and their faces toward the east, and they worshiped the sun toward the east."

It seems, however, that at some stage, some of the

worshippers deliberately snubbed the Holy of Holies and faced the sun, provoking God to warn that he would act against them with fury.

In the Soncino edition of the Bible, Dr. Solomon Fisch's commentary says the following in regard to this passage:

"The entrance to the Temple was on the east side and the Holy of Holies on the west in order to eliminate the popular sun-worship which was practised toward the east. These idolaters turned deliberately in that direction to demonstrate their denial of God and their belief in the sun-god. The Rabbis detect in the seemingly superfluous phrase 'with their backs toward the Temple' a wanton affront of the Divine Presence whose abode is in the west. The Mishnah records that the offending words were recalled during the festival of Tabernacles: 'When the celebrants reached the gate which leads out to the east, they turned their faces from east to west (thus facing the Temple) and said: Our fathers who were in this place stood with their back toward the Temple of the Lord had their faces towards the east, and they worshipped the sun towards the east: but as for us, our eyes are turned to the Lord".

The incident illustrates how it was possible that pagan elements could be brought into the very precincts of the sanctuary, and what shock and horror this caused within traditionalist circles.

By the time Freemasonry developed, however, sun-worship was no longer a threat or concern, and the original east-facing orientation could be emulated in the Lodge.

The three arguments noted above could therefore be used, with the Lodge Master placed in the east "to open the Lodge and employ and instruct the Brethren in Freemasonry".

In his book "The Freemason at Work", Harry Carr addresses the question of why certain Masonic references speak of a Mason moving from west to east, and others of moving from east to west. Utilising 18th century Masonic material, especially a French Masonic catechism, Carr suggests that a Master Mason has two duties – to look to the east for inspirational light, and to turn to the west to spread that light.

There is a chapter about light at the beginning of this book.

13. IMPROPER SOLICITATION

When I joined the Lodge of Israel in England the motivation was personal and came on my own initiative. My father had been a Mason, I knew that a number of clergy were active in the movement though some faith communities remained bitterly opposed, and I had long thought that one day I would find myself showing an interest. I well remember the morning when one of my congregation encountered me in the synagogue precincts and drew the conversation round to the pleasure he got out of his Lodge.

Later I learnt that the craft does not allow canvassing for membership, and the hints I had been given were more or less as far as a Mason could go in trying to lead someone else's mind in the direction of Lodge membership.

Naturally it intrigued me to find that "improper solicitation" was not permitted, especially as I was well aware that a quite different profession regularly engaged in solicitation for improper purposes.

I was not quite certain about what to think of (legal) solicitors, though I heard some people accuse barristers of frequenting the bars too often. This was probably before Horace Rumpole became a television personality. In my youth I studied law, and I have often wondered whether I would have made a success of soliciting or barristering.

I suspect that Freemasonry had good political reasons for its ban on solicitation. In the 17th and early 18th century the movement was engaged in efforts to bring a different climate to society. Strict control was consequently exercised over membership. Those who were likely to be assets to the cause entered by a process of osmosis. We are not certain how many were diplomatically rejected, but there must have been a number.

There was probably some grumbling when James Anderson and his contemporaries articulated a policy of broad religious tolerance, which meant that whoever else was not accepted into the craft, members of non-establishment religions could not be automatically excluded.

An applicant could, as was the situation in my own case, take the hint that his candidature would be welcome, but no-one could be conscripted or dragged in. A person had to be able to say that he came "of his own free will and accord". Rather different from the missionising carried out by many religious denominations who apply spiritual or emotional pressure to people to convert to their particular faiths...

Improper solicitation is still not permitted in the craft, but with declining numbers and the disappearance of the over-strict rules of secrecy, we now have open evenings and even utilise the media to bring our principles and values to the attention of the public.

It possibly is a veiled form of solicitation – but hardly "improper".

However, we still don't pressure anyone to apply. We still expect applicants to choose to come forward and to say, in these or similar words, "Do you think I should join?"

I do not recall the exact contents of my conversation with my congregant Mason all those years ago, but possibly I also said, "Do you think I should join?" I know that I was interviewed by a rather daunting committee and made to feel that Freemasonry was a very prestigious thing. I no longer worry so much about the prestige, but I have never regretted becoming a member. I find it a bit amusing to see that my name and photograph are sometimes used in Masonic publicity campaigns. I seem to have arrived.

14. VOLUME OF THE SACRED LAW

Very nice, say some believers. The Bible is on display in Masonic meeting places! Bible readings are part of Masonic ritual! Bible characters and events punctuate Masonic terminology!

Not so nice at all, say the critics of the craft. These Masons are undermining the official religions! They are setting up in opposition to the churches and confusing people! They even call their meeting places temples because they think they are on a par with the churches and synagogues!

The critics have it all wrong. Freemasonry is religious without being a religion. Can't the United States print "In God We Trust" on their currency notes without being accused of hijacking or kidnapping religion? Aren't legislatures allowed to open with a prayer without being enemies of the faith?

Mackey's *Encyclopedia of Freemasonry* puts it clearly: "Freemasons do not believe that religion ever is or can be a monopoly owned by any church. Religion belongs to man as man. If a man desires to worship he is free to do so where he stands. If workmen wish to pray and worship there is nobody to forbid them; they have as much right to turn the Lodge into an altar as they have to sit or stand or speak" (1946 ed., vol. 3, page 1212).

Any problems we have in relation to the Bible are quite different. Problem: what do non-Judeo-Christians do as Masons? Answer: they can take their obligations on their own Scriptures. Other Scriptures apart from the Bible are honoured in a Lodge room; at my Lodge in Jerusalem there are three holy books on the pedestal, the Hebrew, Christian and Islamic. The Christians don't seem to have an issue with Old Testament material in the ritual, nor do the Muslims, who accept that Masonic culture is built upon Biblical events that do not figure – at least in the same way – in their own tradition.

Problem: how much do we have to believe of the Masonic version of Biblical texts? Some interpretations are influenced by the Jewish Midrash, though even in Judaism such material lacks compulsory status. Other interpretations are pure legend, sometimes probably deliberately constructed in the 17th or 18th century by the founding fathers of the Speculative craft. Masons find it all very interesting but are not compelled to believe it.

Actually something paradoxical has happened here. From the 9th century, Jewish exegesis underwent a radical change. Islam accused Jews of distorting their own Bible, and within Judaism the Karaites alleged that the rabbis had moved away from the Biblical text, so the Massoretes ("keepers of tradition") established a standard Hebrew version, and the classical commentators explained the Scriptures according to plain sense and reason. Some introduced linguistic analogies – e.g. to medieval French - whilst others analysed the Christian interpretations and brought them into their literary polemics.

The authority of Midrashic exposition was downgraded by some commentators, though others found it useful as an aid to devotion and even uncovered layers of mystical underpinning of the text. On the whole, however, this age of interpretation was a rational intellectual era with little time for myths and legends.

Modern Freemasonry came in at the cusp of the medieval and modern periods – and chose to give credence to myths and legends. Nonetheless, the men who established Speculative Masonry were rationalists, scientists and intellectuals. How and why they seized upon or invented myths and legends we cannot be certain. De Saguliers and James Anderson aren't here to ask.

15. HEAL, CONCEAL, REVEAL

Masonic secrets must not be divulged. We try to make the point by means of a rhyming ditty using the three words, *hele, conceal, reveal*. The first word stumps everybody. If it were *heal* we would have no problem: it would fit in with the rhyme, it would come straight out of normal English speech – but it would defeat our purpose.

There must be, and is, an old English word *h-e-l-e* with the sense of hiding or covering up. It doesn't figure at all in my Collins English Dictionary, which means that it has not been part of current English for a very long time. Whence shall my help come?

Another resource, Skeat's Etymological Dictionary, tells me that the word *helm*, meaning armour for the head, is from an Anglo-Saxon root *helan* which means to cover. So *hele* does exist (it is probably the origin of the word *helmet*, which of course means a head covering), and the Oxford English Dictionary further informs me that in the early

Middle Ages it denoted to keep something secret: in the 13th and 14th centuries it had the specialised meaning of covering something with earth, slates or tiles.

This building connotation seems like an indication that the word was part of the original technical vocabulary of Operative Masonry, and was brought into the Speculative version of the craft a few centuries later.

The original pronunciation may have been *hale*, rhyming with *bale*, *male*, *shale* and *ale*, but it seems to have been pronounced to rhyme with *conceal* and *reveal* from at least the 17th century, as is borne out in a series of Masonic documents.

The craft has been exercised by this archaic word for generations. Thousands of candidates have entered upon their Masonic careers puzzled that no-one has explained to them what was going on. The lack of explanation cannot be blamed on the Worshipful Master who himself has never had the history of the word explained to him. Maybe we need to give more attention to in-service courses for Lodge Masters.

When I was a candidate for initiation I was so overawed by the whole procedure that I simply repeated what I was told to repeat. In due course I saw many others in the same situation. When I became a Lodge Master myself, I did what was expected of me, because I didn't have an alternative.

So what should we do now? I am sure that every jurisdiction has a Ritual Committee. I believe they should urgently take the problem on board and consider drafting a few words that can be used in the Lodge room to make things clear to the candidate and the rest of the Lodge, and give appropriate guidance to the Worshipful Master. It might help to go back to an early 18th century precedent and use the phrase "hide and conceal", or at least for the Master to comment as an aside, "The old-fashioned word *hele* means to hide."

Hele is not the only archaic word we use in Freemasonry, but the others don't seem to give us such difficulties, though many parts of our ritual are hard for Lodge Masters – not to speak of candidates - who are not native English speakers and can hardly get their tongues around the ornate phraseology of King-James-Version English.

16. FELLOW TRAVELLERS

I joined the Jewish fraternal order of B'nai B'rith as a member of the First Lodge of England fifty years ago. I liked it and eventually headed the adult education committee of the movement in the United Kingdom. I retained my B'nai B'rith involvement when I moved to Australia; later I joined the English-speaking BB Lodge in Jerusalem, which eventually closed down for lack of leadership, though I argued (fruitlessly) for its activities to continue.

I am well aware of the quasi-Masonic ritual of B'nai B'rith (I even rewrote some of its Australian version) and know that it borrows craft terminology to articulate its ethos – light, justice, peace, benevolence, brotherly (and sisterly) love, harmony and truth. BB does not deny that its 19th century founders in the United States adopted and adapted Masonic material, so the similarities are more than accidental... though only in B'nai B'rith am I entitled to call my wife my Sister.

The historians are, however, not certain about the many

other fraternities that have operated throughout history, a few functioning continuously but many rising and declining like the gourd that "came up in a night and perished in a night" (Jonah 4:10). Is there a historical link or mutual influence between these movements and Freemasonry?

The fact that they all tended to have a sense of brotherhood and community, a set of membership criteria, a system of rank and degrees, a rite of initiation, a philosophy and quasi-catechism, an interest in alchemy and science, a collection of legendary tales and a claim to ancient lineage, as well as phraseology that emphasises brotherly love, relief and truth, neither proves - nor disproves - cross-fertilisation.

In some cases, however, we can trace a clear connection with Freemasonry. Examples are the Rosicrucians and the Asiatic Brethren.

The Rosicrucians arose in central Europe in the early 17th century and in some ways moulded and were themselves remoulded by Freemasonry to such an extent that long before the establishment of the first Grand Lodge in England a literary work could say, "We are Brethren of the Rosie Cross: We have the Mason Word and second sight."

By way of contrast the Asiatic Brethren arose in Vienna in 1780 and hardly lasted a decade. They practised a strange combination of Jewish and Christian kabbalistic ideas spiced with sexual symbolism. The historian Jacob Katz calls the movement "a kind of imitation, or travesty, of the Freemasons".

The scholars of Freemasonry have delved into countless other movements ranging from the Natufians to the Templars and asked the right questions. But it is not only historical links or the lack of them that need to be traced but how and why the Masonic craft survived when so many other groups went under.

For my part there is a further – and probably much more urgent and topical – question to be asked. I ask this question not as a historian or even as a Mason but as a confused human being living in a complex and difficult era. If brotherly love, relief and truth were and are the centrepiece of so many movements including Freemasonry, how did they all fail to re-make civilisation on the broad principles which they all shared?

There are many possible answers. I guess mine is cynical: if they did not profoundly improve society, at least they may have stopped it getting worse.

17. DUE AT A BARMITZVAH

A Jewish boy earns the status of Barmitzvah when he is 13 and in a religious sense enters upon the obligations of adulthood (the equivalent for girls is Batmitzvah at the age of 12). The occasion usually goes with a party. At a certain Barmitzvah celebration in Sydney I was seated next to the boy's father, a lifelong Mason, and our conversation turned to Masonic terminology, especially the question of whether the ritual should say, "every Brother has received *his due*" – or "*his dues*".

We didn't solve the problem but we recognised that variations in Masonic rites could be discussed endlessly.

Next morning I looked up the source of the word "due" and found that it is from a Latin root which means "to owe" and is connected in theme and origin with "duty". In the sense of money which is owed, it is connected with "debt" and "debit". Your *dues* are the money that you owe or that is owed to you. Your *due* is the respectful treatment that is your legal and moral right.

In both senses the word has an important role in Freemasonry.

In Operative Freemasonry, working Masons were of course entitled to their set wages (in 1350 a master Freemason in England received four pence and other masons three pence), and there are Masonic legends of how such wages were assessed and paid during the building of King Solomon's Temple. In Speculative Freemasonry, brethren receive no pay – other than the satisfaction their membership brings them and the work they do for the community - but they are duty-bound to pay membership dues for the upkeep of the Lodge and of Grand Lodge.

Since working together in peace and harmony was and remains essential in a Masonic community, occasions of conflict must be prevented. In the Middle Ages there was a mechanism for mediation conducted on the Master's behalf by the Wardens – a pioneering exercise in industrial relations, probably paralleled across the gamut of medieval guilds. Members would not be able to work together if grudges were allowed to ferment, so it was important to see that "every Brother has received his due".

The need and ways to work for internal harmony within a Lodge are discussed in the chapter on "At Variance" earlier in this book.

Some Masonic writings combine the two senses of "due" in a commitment "to pay the men their wages and see that every brother has had his due".

Of course we know and use the word *due* in other senses too – for example, ensuring that a Lodge is *duly* constituted, declaring that the orientation of the Lodge is *due* east and west, and – in some rites - referring to a *Due* Guard, though the phrase probably originated as *Dieu Garde*, "God keep".

This phrase indicates the influence of French Masons and terminology in the creation of the craft. Even the word Freemason may derive from French, from *Frère Macon* or *Francmacon,* though there are other theories, including the idea that the mason belonged to an "emancipated" trade (franc-me(s)tier) unlike a labourer or plasterer.

I recall the Barmitzvah party conversation about "due" and "dues" because in *due* course the erstwhile Barmitzvah boy became a Freemason himself... and ended up marrying my daughter.

18. GOD - A FREEMASON?

As I sit in Lodge I glance at the letter "G" suspended from the ceiling. The "G" is for God. That "G" is a fixed point in my life. Whilst "G" is in place the world is in order. Browning said, "God's in His heaven – all's right with the world".

Which God? That depends on one's cultural baggage. A Jewish, a Christian, a Muslim God? The Jew thinks of Him with a Jewish mindset, the Christian with a Christian mindset, the Muslim with an Islamic one. God in Himself is un-adjectival.

That God is pure spirit without physical form is so axiomatic that we wonder how the Bible can say anything different. But it still does. The 15th chapter of the Book of Exodus attaches descriptions to His name. "The Lord is a warrior" it says at the beginning of the chapter, and at the end, "I the Lord am Your physician".

Biblical commentary insists that such descriptions are not to be taken literally They do not tell us what God *is* but what He *does*. He is a warrior, because when justice is denied He fights for it: He cannot remain uninvolved. He is a physician, because when man is suffering pain He provides herbs that have medicinal properties, He endows the doctors with skill, He strengthens the patient's will to live and their courage to bear.

What does He mean for Freemasons?

Scripture does not claim that "God is a Freemason", at least not in so many words.

But it does use building-trade verbs about Him. He creates, He plans, He designs, He forms, He builds, He constructs.

Cawdray's *Treasurie of Similies* published in 1609 quotes an earlier source, *A Spiritual and Most Precious Perle* by Werdmuller, published in 1550.

"As the Free-Mason heweth the hard stones," it says, "even so God the Heavenly Free-Mason buildeth a Christian Church". Note the 16th century use of the term Freemason, which in fact was also known at least as early as the 14th century, two hundred years earlier.

The term "free" must have a building connotation – either *the builder* was free in some sense, or *his materials* were free, i.e. freestone as against rough-stone.

But that's not my point here. Much can be and has been said by the scholars about the origins of the name Freemason. The quotation from Werdmuller proves that Operative Freemasonry was largely engaged in the erection of church buildings, many of which have withstood the battering of time and the elements, and still remain in place after so many centuries.

For our present purpose what is significant is the analogy between God and the Freemason. From the suspended "G" in the Lodge room we learn that the Mason must know *what* he is building, and *why* and *how*.

Is the Mason building for his own glory, or for God's? Look at Psalm 49 for a warning of what can happen to those who think their palaces will stand for ever and assure them of immortality.

Is he building carefully? Does he put in an honest day's work? Does he treat his co-workers fairly? Does he sacrifice his family for the sake of his business or status? At the end of the day can he face his own conscience?

When I sit in Lodge and look upwards I know I am under scrutiny by the Divine Foreman. When one day He asks me about myself, I hope I can give an adequate answer.

19. THE STARS ABOVE

Some Masonic buildings have nondescript ceilings with little or no artistic value. Other Masonic ceilings, often painted navy blue, have innumerable little stars, sometimes made of gold leaf.

How I know these stars are innumerable has to do with some of my less successful Masonic moments when I found my attention wandering and sat there trying to count the stars. I never completed the task, partly because I kept making mistakes and going back to Square One (a phrase which could have a craft as well as a sporting significance), partly because eventually the Lodge procedures reclaimed my attention, and my time to daydream was over.

The way we generally explain the star-studded ceiling is that it symbolises Creation as described in the Volume of the Sacred Law, in Genesis Chapter 1. First there was "darkness upon the face of the deep" (the navy blue background) and then God said, "Let there be light" (the stars) – a drama familiar to every Freemason from the moment of his initiation.

Light, as an earlier chapter in this book explains, is a central symbol - not only in Freemasonry but in the cultures of many peoples. One of the ambitions of the faithful Mason is to help lead mankind out of the confusion and uncertainty of moral and mental darkness towards the light that glimmers faintly like the little stars but hopefully will grow and develop as a guide to thinking and action.

When did Masonic buildings first have starry ceilings?

There are two answers.

When Lodges met in other people's buildings, generally public houses, there was little opportunity of influencing the design of the rooms that were rented for craft meetings (there were sometimes disputes over the amount the Lodge paid the landlords and the adequacy of the room they were allotted, and some Lodges had to migrate from public house to public house).

But when the craft began to acquire its own premises it was a different story. Masonic catechisms from the early 18th century included a question of how high a Lodge was – perhaps metaphorically – and the answer had to do with the height of the starry heavens.

A more direct connection with the stars entered the ritual when Lodge rooms were decorated with canopies and with a representation of the Blazing Star, probably in reference to the New Testament phrase, "I am the bright and morning star" (Revelations 22:16).

Tracing Board illustrations and explanations, however, commonly refer to the star-studded canopy of heaven and link the stars in the ceiling to the Creation story, adding that when human beings gaze at the skies and stars they find themselves awestruck at the majesty and glory of the Creator – a theme found in many parts of Biblical poetry, notably Psalm 19:2.

The philosopher Immanuel Kant, a contemporary of many 18th century Masonic pioneers, saw the best evidence of God in the majesty of the heavens and the greatness of the human moral conscience.

It is not only Masonic buildings that have star-studded decor. It is typical of a range of public buildings ranging from town halls and law courts to Jewish synagogues – even some Christian churches.

20. SIGNS AND SYMBOLS

Despite the time and interest I have always devoted to Freemasonry, religion was my day job. I spent 45 years in the pulpit and continue to engage in religious research from a more academic point of view. I even give occasional sermons.

Sometimes I get personal compliments: someone recently said about me in an article that I was an iconic rabbi. I felt bucked but a bit bewildered, since I am not sure what is expected of an icon.

Yet I know that icons are not objects of worship but symbols. If I am in some sense iconic, I should like to think that I symbolise faith, decency, reasonability, justice and good citizenship.

Masonry is full of symbols and signs but they don't always get a fair deal from outsiders who find it ridiculous that grown men wear aprons, parade in processions and perform rituals. Some critics even think we ride around the Lodge room on goats.

I have news for the critics. Whoever they are, whatever they do, they too live by rituals, probably without realising it. In religion certainly – but also in parliament and the courts, in social and sports clubs, in the polling booths and pubs, on the buses and even in the butcher's shop. Everywhere there are set ways of doing things, procedures that must be followed.

You can accuse Freemasons of overdoing the ritual, but have you ever been to a board meeting peopled by pedants?

You can accuse Freemasons of making secret signs, but have you ever been to an auction sale and seen the chemistry between auctioneers and bidders?

The rituals of Freemasonry are a means of identification. They show that you are one of the group. They symbolise what the group stands for. They are the poetry that brings richness and feeling into craft membership.

Human beings need signs, symbols and rituals. If life were supra-rational and man no more than a disembodied soul, it might be possible to live on an ethereal plane – but that's not the reality. We are body as well as soul – and we live on several levels at once. We inhabit the world of ideas, and also the world of phenomena. We link the two by means of symbolic signs and ceremonies.

Whoever you are, whatever you do, you cannot escape the signs and symbols that plant you in your place and time.

Freemasonry doesn't make its ceremonies into an idol to be worshipped but an icon that symbolises great teachings and values.

We try to make our ceremonies dignified and distinctive, especially when we are on public show, for instance at a Masonic funeral. Sloppy performance of our rituals loses us credibility – and it gives the critics unnecessary ammunition. I have known in my time quite a number of great Masonic ritualists who were an example and an inspiration. It requires careful training, preparation and concentration to be a good ritualist.

It is a pity that outsiders see so little of what we do for the community. Masonic processions were once part of the landscape, and public buildings were opened with a parade of Masons in regalia. These days the only public Masonic presence many people see is at memorial services for the dead. What about our work *for the living*? Our charity work? Our involvement in flood and fire relief? What we do for old people and children? This is how we put Masonic ideals to work in the community.

21. APPLES AND PLUMBS

A lot of things set off a writer's memories, perhaps because as a person gets older they tend to reminisce and ramble. Once I decided to write a chapter on plumb rules and plumb lines I remembered that when I got a certain rabbinical position in London years ago, someone said, "Apple has a plum job." Why a prestigious position is a plum job I am not sure; there must have been a time when the plum was regarded as a superior species of fruit.

Obviously plums and plumbs are not the same thing at all, but there is a similarity of sound. So enough already of the plums...now let's focus on plumbs.

A plumb is a weight (usually lead) suspended by a line. Its purpose is to determine the water level, hence the name "plumber" for the tradesman who deals with problems involving water. The word is from Latin "*plumbum*", lead. Another word derived from the same source is the Yiddish "*blombe*" or "*plombe*", a lead seal that testifies that a meat product is *kosher*. Metaphorically, to plumb, as a verb, means to investigate something strange or difficult. Any expert learns to plumb the depths of his or her subject.

Freemasonry – Operative as well as Speculative - lays great store on geometry as the leading component of the science of building. Everything has to be well designed. Everything has to be measured, both the horizontal and the vertical. The Mason has to be the master of his working tools. Each implement has a distinct purpose and role and has to be handled with appropriate skill and expertise.

Samuel Prichard, author of "Masonry Dissected", published in 1730, explains that the square is "to lay down true and right lines", the level "to try all horizontals" and the plumb rule is "to try all uprights".

Moral lessons are derived from each, because Freemasonry believes in building a sound structure of human character, so the idea of the plumb line teaches Freemasons to measure situations and adjust their conduct to the proper level.

This is a valid point - but it's not what is indicated in the vision of the Biblical prophet Amos, who in Chapter 7 of his Book (verses 7 and 8) writes the following, which is actually quoted in our Masonic ritual: "Thus He showed me, and behold, the Lord stood beside a wall made by a plumbline, with a plumbline in His hand. And the Lord said to me, 'Amos, what do you see?' And I said, 'A plumbline'. Then said the Lord, 'Behold, I will set a plumbline in the midst of My people Israel: I will not again pardon them any more'."

The statement that the wall was "made by a plumbline" but now needs to be checked suggests that initially it was built correctly but is now beginning to totter and collapse – an allusion to the people of Israel deviating from the norms established by the Creator. God, it seems, is no longer prepared to forgive the people, and the prophet recognises that there is no longer any point in trying to speak in their defence.

Our Operative Masonic ancestors, for all their experience and expertise, must have had times of great disappointment. They used their plumblines and whatever other measuring tools were available, but their work sometimes had to be knocked down and re-started from scratch. Did they ever deliberately botch the job or fail to follow instructions? Who knows? We can only surmise. We hope their Masters never gave up on them but encouraged them to try again and learn from their mistakes.

22. WHERE YOU LODGE

In Chapter 1 of the Book of Ruth, a brave young woman says to her mother-in-law Naomi, "Where you go I will go: where you lodge I will lodge". The historical context is not really our concern in this collection of Masonic essays, but the word "lodge" is. It shows that the base meaning of "lodge" is to dwell.

In that sense the medieval stonemasons who were away from home for long periods were accommodated near their work site; there they lodged, ate, gathered, chatted and became a fellowship. The storehouse where they kept their material and tools was also called a lodge.

The Operative Masons were not all rough, illiterate labourers. There must have been thinkers, artists, musicians and even scholars amongst them. A notable group were the Comatines, builders and architects from Como who fled the Barbarian invasion of Rome and went on to found *collegia* of builders in many parts of Continental Europe.

Schools and universities came to have lodges, generally

with a security function – the porter's lodge, the gatekeeper's lodge, etc. The fortunate owners of large manor houses also had lodges at the entrance of the driveway to keep an official eye on who entered and who left the property.

The uses to which the word "lodge" was put were legion. The Latin *logia,* probably denoting a gallery, became the Italian *loggia*, a balcony in a theatre.

In Speculative Freemasonry the lodge came to be two things in one – a place and a group of people. A similar dichotomy of language applies to words like club and church. "I'm going to the Club" denotes a place; "I am a club member" indicates a social group. Someone who says, "I have to tidy the church", is talking about a building; "It's part of Church doctrine" indicates an *ecclesia*, a group of believers.

Modern-day Masons have two issues – how to maintain Lodge buildings at a time of declining membership, and how to enhance the Lodge as a fellowship. We seem to have too many buildings for current needs; many require more refurbishment than we can afford. Fortunately Grand Lodge attention is constantly directed to both aspects.

But how do you enhance the feeling of fellowship that makes disparate individuals into a Lodge? The human make-up of the membership needs to be looked at – the age range, the ethnic spectrum, the socio-economic spread. All should be on our agenda. We know that differences between people are not meant to matter within the Lodge or to intrude upon membership unity, but can't we consciously try to create a varied Lodge and then be smart enough to manage it without dissension and in harmony?

A second thought. Can't we do more to keep in touch with all our members, not just sending them formal notices of meetings but sharing their achievements and interests, their joys and sorrows? If people drop out of sight because they claim "no-one cared", there has been a distinct failure on the part of Lodge management.

Can we streamline and improve our Lodge meetings - and enhance the quality of the after-meeting suppers? Often the catering is slipshod and we would probably be better off without it. Whatever we do should have class and elegance.

I am upset to think that sometimes outsiders laugh at us. I am ashamed that some of our own members laugh at us too. A fresh look at who we are and what we do might give our movement more style, excitement and cohesion. Let's derive a new slogan from the Book of Ruth – "Your Lodge is my Lodge!"

23. LEMECH AND TUBAL-CAIN

Freemasonry has an understandable fascination with a whole range of Biblical characters who played a role as builders, artisans or architects. Many of these figures get a mention in the craft ritual.

A notable exception is Betzalel ("In the Shadow of God"), the chief designer and master craftsman of the Tabernacle in the wilderness (Exodus 31:2). His omission has always upset me, not just because fair's fair and he should be acknowledged, but because my father's father, who lived in Jerusalem, had the name Betzalel and my parents named me Betzalel in Hebrew in his honour, though in English I am Raymond.

Fortunately, due recognition is given to Tubal-Cain or Tuval-Kayin ("Flowing Forth of Cain"), who "forged instruments of copper and iron". He is referred to in Genesis Chapter 4. The first four chapters of Genesis introduce us to all the basic features of human civilisation – creation, conflict, clothing, culture, climate, procreation, poetry, religion, rebellion, agriculture, animals, apples... The son of Lemech and Tzillah, Tuval-Kayin was the pioneer of work in metals. His first name is from the Hebrew root *yaval*, to bring or produce. His second name, Cain – strictly speaking Kayin (the root means to acquire or repair) – was the son of Adam and Eve.

According to the rabbinic commentators, Tuval-Kayin "mended" the sin of the original Cain, who killed his brother Abel (in Hebrew *Hevel*, with the accent on the first syllable). This comment seems to have a theological dimension in that the sins of the fathers (see the Ten Commandments in Exodus 20) do not automatically blight the lives of their children so long as the latter perform good deeds that rehabilitate the family name.

Lemech (it is ungrammatical to call him Lamech apart from at the end of a Biblical phrase or sentence where a "pausal" form is required: another example is Japhet, who is ordinarily called Yefet) may come from a Semitic root that means powerful. Some see it as a metathesis of *Melech* (king).

In these words the "ch" sound is as in the Scottish "loch" (not as in "rich"; nor is it a "k" as in "kin").

There may have been two Lemechs (if there was only one, we have two genealogical narratives):

- The son of Methusaleh (correctly Metushellach, with the accent on "shell"). This Lemech lived to be 777 and was the father of No'ach.
- The son of Metusha'el, the husband of Adah

and Tzillah, the father of Yaval, Yuval, Tuval-
Kayin and their sister Na'amah.

Through his children, Lemech was the progenitor of domestic and pastoral life (Yaval was the inventor of tents and animal husbandry); musicians (Yuval invented musical instruments); and artisans (Tuval-Kayin invented metal implements).

In post-Biblical works such as the Book of Jubilees, Lemech himself played an important role in civilisation when he transmitted the tradition of his grandfather Enoch (Hanoch) to his son No'ach. Enoch was said to be a pious, scholarly man and the inventor of literacy, the author of prophetic letters which were preserved by No'ach during the Flood.

For more information on the preservation of the ancient records, I refer you to the chapter in this book on China and the Masonic Archives.

24. ALL GLORY TO THE MOST HIGH

In the 1960s when I was living in Britain there was immense national controversy about the Bishop of Woolwich's book, "Honest to God". The author, Bishop John AT Robinson, was accused of being a heretic because he told his readers to re-examine the conventional language and assumptions of traditionalist faith.

Some thought he was undermining religion. The truth is that for the first time in many churchgoers' lives they were being challenged to use their heads and think. Until then, religious issues had probably never (not even in the days of Darwin) occupied so much of the media and of the mindset of the British people. Now everyone – even the atheists - had an opinion about where God was... "Up There"... "Out There"... "In Here"...

In Freemasonry we seem to have our own answer, even though the craft is not a religion or denomination and has no theology, requiring only that a Mason should have a general belief in a Supreme Being. We do have a ritual reference to God as the Most High, which seems to indicate that we attribute to God a spatial location and that we agree that He is "Up There", whatever the phrase may mean.

The Bible uses the same epithet for God when it calls Him *Elyon*, The Most High One (Psalm 91:1), and entreats Him, "Look down from Heaven, Your holy dwelling" (Deuteronomy 26:15). It says that Moses *ascended* to God and the Almighty *came down* on Mount Sinai (Exodus 19:3,18). It avers that Heaven is His throne and earth His footstool (Isaiah 66:1).

How can any of this be possible if God is not physical and cannot be pinned down to a location? It is part of anthropomorphism, which is human language that is used to characterise the Almighty. Because our earthly vocabulary is insufficient, we have no choice but to use human terminology for God, but we know not to take it literally. It is poetry. It is metaphor. It indicates; it does not define.

The real truth cannot be captured. The moment we can hold God in our hand we reduce and limit Him. We make ourselves so powerful that we reverse the roles: man becomes God and God becomes man.

We have to recognise that we are using poetic language. Referring to God as the Most High is not a matter of *where* He is but *what* He is. His pre-eminence and perfection are infinitely above ours. As Hebrew liturgical authors put it, He is *Melech Elyon*, the Most High King, in contrast to man, who is *Melech Evyon,* the lowly "king".

Louis Jacobs says this dichotomy "has been criticised for

its poor opinion of man, robbing him of his dignity, (but note that) it is puny, insignificant man who recognises the majesty of God."

Freemasonry knew when it introduced into its ritual the cry, "All Glory to the Most High!", that man is a lowly being who has the capacity to make himself great. He can raise himself from the gutter and aspire to the stars. He will never completely get there, but he will ascend higher than the cynic who says it isn't even worth trying.

Don't look to Freemasonry for theological lessons, for credos and confessions. Instead value it for its *realism*: its acknowledgement that man is puny in comparison to God, and its *optimism*: little man can build himself and his earth-bound world into a heaven-bent temple.

25. MASONIC ORIGINS

There is no definitive answer as to how Freemasonry originated. The little documentary material we have is patchy and inconclusive. The result is little certainty and a great deal of conjecture. There are several leading theories, but all have their major difficulties.

The view of Rev. James Anderson, the formulator of the first Masonic Books of Constitutions, is that the craft grew up with Biblical man. Whether Anderson believed his own rather fanciful stories we cannot be sure, but he was roundly attacked in his own lifetime, and later generations of historians attach little credence to what he wrote.

The strange thing is that there are leading Freemasons who still tell me that the craft goes back to Adam and Eve or at least to Noah and Nimrod. For them the unlikelihood of the story being true has never got in the way of Anderson-like myths and legends.

There is a view that Freemasonry began in the days when King Solomon and his supporters built the Temple in

Jerusalem, but this is more allegorical than accurate. Since the craft focussed on the art of building, it was thought that there had to be an ancient prototype. It is not impossible that the men who worked on the Temple had a trade association, but we cannot be certain. In any case it is unlikely that Solomon, though the sponsor of the project, would have been the Grand Master of the workers' group.

One of the more credible theories grounds Freemasonry in the guilds of medieval stonemasons, whose craft could have died out once the great building projects were completed by about 1540, had they not begun to accept "honorary" or "gentleman" Masons who were fascinated by the Operative Masons' philosophising about their trade, changed its character, and eventually took over the whole movement.

Some scholars question whether the medieval stonemasons were ever organised into guilds or other corporate bodies, though it would be strange if they were not, bearing in mind that they worked, lived and probably moved in distinctive groups, and that there are records of a range of other artisans' guilds including carpenters.

A second reasonable theory looks at the rise of Enlightenment man and his search for scientific and ethical truths upon which to revamp European society, and posits that this more gentrified and educated group adopted the remnants of the Operative Masonic system as a structure and perhaps as a facade that disarmed critics by giving the appearance of a long-standing institution.

A major drawback to both theories is that everything is rather too tidy, implying that either the workers or the thinkers were all of one mind and made united policy decisions about future directions for their group.

Another drawback is that there is hardly any evidence of English Lodges accepting non-operative members, though the situation is marginally different in Scotland. Since we are dealing with relatively recent times the lack of written records is odd. It is however possible that it suited both groups to keep their affairs secret.

It is likely that there was a great deal of discussion, dissension and restlessness in each group and it took a long time for things to settle into a solid reality. For some time there may have been a period of parallel existence, in which Operative and Speculative Freemasonry lived side by side before finally merging.

Thus if we are forced to decide which of these two main theories is the more correct, the best answer is probably "both".

www.ingramcontent.com/pod-product-compliance
Lightning Source LLC
Chambersburg PA
CBHW020341290526
45785CB00005B/2130

THE RAPE THAT LASTED A LIFETIME

Does It Ever End?

JODI MORLEY

outskirts
press